D0905685

# The Lost Art of Baking with Yeast & Pastries

## Delicious Hungarian Cakes

By

Photography by ...ayes

RHYW

# Copyright Page from the Original Book

Published by Black Inc.
an imprint of Schwartz Media Pty Ltd
Level 5, 289 Flinders Lane
Melbourne Victoria 3000 Australia
email: enquiries@blackincbooks.com
http://www.blackincbooks.com

National Library of Australia Cataloguing-in-Publication entry

Schwartz, Baba.
The lost art of baking with yeast:
delicious Hungarian cakes and pastries.

ISBN 1 86395 259 4.

1. Cake. 2. Pastry. 3. Bagels. I. Title.

641.865

ReadHowYouWant partners with publishers to provide books for ALL Kinds of Readers. For more information about Becoming A (RHYW) Registered Reader and to find more titles in your preferred format, visit:

<u>www.readhowyouwant.com</u>

# TABLE OF CONTENTS

# DEDICATION & ACKNOWLEDGEMENTS

I wish to dedicate this book to my family and friends. To all those who make me believe that I can bake well.

First amongst them is my husband Bandi, a connoisseur from way back. His mother was matchless when it came to baking. I am not sure that I equal her talents but I have tried and am still trying. This is why his praise is so precious.

Our three sons took the goodies for granted. If you can eat them every week, what's so special about them? It was different for their friends. Somehow they found out when my *rózsas* were ready. They always arrived at the right time, acting as if they were 'just passing by'. They only admitted later that they had come by design. So my three boys started to consider themselves lucky. They told me so and gave me the pleasure of their appreciation.

Our sons married and presented us with lovely daughters. Later, the grandchildren arrived. I want to thank them all for the many (multiply this many) compliments, applause, accolades and praise that I have received for my baking.

My friends often use my recipes and relate to me the triumphs they achieve. This also makes me feel good. Friends, thank you.

My mother baked the best cakes in the whole wide world. My aim is to achieve her degree of mastery over the baking board.

I would like to thank my son and publisher, Morry Schwartz, without whom this book would never have come about, Silvia Kwon and Sophy Williams at Black Inc., Meera Freeman, for taking the Hungarian accent out of the original manuscript, Thomas Deverall, for design and layout, and Sonia Payes, for her expert photography.

# PREFACE

Some of my most poignant childhood memories take me back to my Savta's kitchen and to the many happy hours spent with her there, baking – learning to knead, roll, cut and, of course, taste. I remember the malty smell of the yeast, the joy of watching the rising dough and the skilful hands of my grandmother shaping leftovers into special little shapes for me to bake and eat.

The irony of my grandmother publishing a cookbook will be obvious to anyone who has spent a day baking with her. There is no order to what Savta does – no rules, no measurements, no ingredient that is completely irreplaceable and no system. I have sat, many times, trying to absorb and retain Savta's methods. I have even tried with paper and pen but the constant scurrying to and fro for pinches of salt here and spoons of sugar there, and the casual transfers from bowl to bowl, make it impossible. Every time I watch the same cake being baked it is done slightly differently so I have realised there really are no rules. This book should be a guide, not a bible, because my Savta's baking requires feeling, intuition and adaptation.

Baking at my grandmother's, and indeed, in most households, has always been about so much more than making cakes. The process of mixing and stirring, tasting and adapting is about tradition and brings both my grandmother and those around her great satisfaction. Of course, the joy in my grandmother's cooking lies in the product as much (or to some, arguably more) as in the process. There is nothing in the world better than arriving at my Savta's on a Friday afternoon and being served *rózsa* still warm from the oven with a cup of tea. And for my Savta, there seems to be no greater pride than to watch us relish every mouthful. There have been many occasions when, on journeys back from her house, entire batches of *pogdcsa* have been consumed in the car before we have arrived home. Somehow, Savta's cakes keep getting better and better and resolutions made conscientiously at family dinners to make slice number five the last one are just as conscientiously forgotten.

May this book bring into your household some of this happiness as well as the memories, smells and tastes that I have grown up with. Baking with yeast is a gift that I hope my Savta can impart to you. Baking with yeast is a lost art, and Savta is my family's Michelangelo.

Thea Schwartz, 2003

# Introduction

The aim of this book is to introduce you to yeast, a living organism with many special and wondrous properties, and to demystify the process of baking with yeast.

Many people are apprehensive about working with this marvellous product which, since time immemorial, has been of such great use to humanity. I would like to dispel any fears you may have and convert you into a cook who will both enjoy working with yeast and succeed in mastering its use. I have no doubt that, in a short time, you will come to love and trust in it as much as I do.

Yeast is a minute plant which grows by feeding on carbohydrates: sugar and starch. As it grows, it produces gas as a by-product. This same gas is produced by other rising agents, but the taste and texture of a cake baked with yeast is so different that, for some recipes, there is simply no substitute.

Over the years, I have met accomplished cooks who are reluctant to bake with yeast, only because they have never had the opportunity to experiment with it or use it. Admittedly, the preparation of a good yeast cake does take time and some experience is required. In my native Hungary, yeast is a common product used every day. Every home maker and cook is familiar with yeast and knows how to harness its special properties to prepare a great variety of sweet or savoury cakes and pastries.

So, let me take you by the hand and initiate you in the secrets of my recipes, formulae that have been tried and tested a thousand times. Be assured that, with a minimum of perseverance and practice, you will soon be the proud and praised baker of many delicious creations.

Imagine chocolate rolls, chocolate roses, cheese or jam turnovers, yeast doughnuts, golden dumpling cake, nut and poppy seed rolls and crescents, even yeast meringue rolls. All of these and more will soon grace your table to the delight of your family and friends.

# The Essentials

## INGREDIENTS

### Yeast

The Essentials

Baker's yeast, commonly sold as fresh yeast, can be bought from health-food stores and continental delicatessens. It is also available from the delicatessen department of most supermarkets.

Dry yeast is also reliable and simple to use. Each sachet contains 7g of dry yeast. As it is more concentrated than fresh yeast, each 20g of fresh yeast can be replaced by 1 sachet of dry yeast. Some cookbooks recommend using double this amount but I find that too much yeast does nothing to enhance either the texture or flavour of the baked product.

## Flour

Use the best quality unbleached plain flour. As this is much more expensive than ordinary plain flour, you may choose to keep some of the cheaper product on hand for dusting your dough and work surface.

## Fat

Most European pastries are made with butter.

In my kosher Jewish kitchen, it is forbidden to mix meat with dairy products and, if I want to serve a cake after a festive dinner containing meat, I will make the cake with margarine or oil instead of butter. If you wish to cut down on animal fats because of high cholesterol levels or other health concerns, you can use half butter and half margarine.

Butter used can be salted or unsalted. When using margarine, however, make sure that it is unsalted.

Vegetable oils should be light and without strong flavours – corn, safflower, grapeseed or canola oils are all suitable.

## Sugar

When using white sugar in a recipe, I invariably use caster sugar which is finer than normal granulated sugar and therefore dissolves more readily. To make vanilla sugar, simply split a fresh vanilla bean and store it in your jar of caster sugar. You can keep topping up the jar as the strong perfume of the vanilla bean will go a very long way.

Where brown sugar is specified, use light brown sugar (sometimes called raw sugar).

Icing sugar is very fine and most suitable for dusting the tops of cakes and cookies.

## Nuts and Seeds

I often fill my yeast cakes with various types of ground nuts as well as ground poppy seed. It is handy to have stock of these products available at all times in case the urge to bake should arise unexpectedly.

Raw or ground nuts and ground poppy seed can all be kept in the freezer for quite a long time. They must, however, be stored in airtight containers before freezing.

Poppy seeds are very tough and should therefore be ground before being used to fill cakes. Some delicatessens will grind poppy seed for you on the spot. Some cooks boil poppy seed in milk, causing it to lose its shiny black colour and turn a dull grey. Cooking it in water will preserve its colour.

## Lemon Rind

Freeze the halves of squeezed lemons so that you always have them on hand when you need lemon rind. If you remove them from the freezer 5 minutes before grating, they will yield very finely grated rind.

## Cheese

All cottage cheese specified in this book is the kind sold in block form, tightly packed in plastic. It is more compressed and therefore not as wet as the same product sold in tubs. It is available in both full- and low-fat varieties.

If using low-fat cheese, a few tablespoons of low-fat sour cream will improve its flavour.

## Jam

Apricot jam, used in many of the recipes, should be smooth rather than chunky. Warming the jam slightly will make it easier to spread. Dense plum jam or *powidl* is available from continental delicatessens.

## Sour Cream

Either full- or low-fat sour cream may be used according to your preference.

# EQUIPMENT

## Kneading Tools

An electric mixer equipped with a dough hook and K beater makes kneading easier.

The dough hook is used for kneading soft mixtures whereas the K beater is used for stiffer doughs.

The K beater on minimum speed can be used for working fat into flour to the 'coarse breadcrumb' stage. Speed 3–4 is ideal for kneading.

# Baking Tins

I bake my *kugelhopfs* in the round fluted ring tins specially designed for this purpose. They double as tins for baking my filled chocolate and poppy seed rolls. These rolls can also be baked in narrow high-sided loaf tins. Your pastries will be higher if the dough is contained and supported as it rises.

You will need baking pans with sides for your small pastries and slices, and baking sheets for your cookies.

# Pastry Board

A large pastry board is highly recommended for rolling out and shaping dough. It can be made from a piece of laminated board which is practical and easy to clean. An ideal size is 75–80x50–60cm – the larger the better. If you don't have a pastry board, use a large, clean cloth sprinkled with flour and spread over your work top. This, however, is not the most ideal surface as it is likely to wrinkle whilst you are working.

# Dough Scraper

A plastic dough scraper is practical for cleaning your work surface before wiping it down. You can also use it to scrape the dough from your hands.

## Pastry Brush

A pastry brush is necessary for applying washes to your pastry before baking.

## Cookie Cutters

A selection of different sized cutters are handy as their sharp surfaces ensure ease of cutting. If you have no cutters, a wine glass can be used.

## Ravioli Cutting Wheels

These cutters with their handle and revolving wheel make cutting out strips or squares easy.

They are available with both straight and fancy blades.

## Baking Paper

Lining your baking tins or sheets with baking paper creates a clean, non-stick surface. It dispenses with the need to grease the baking dishes and makes washing up easier too.

If you are using round or fancy tins which are difficult to line, simply spray them with oil from a spray can.

# Principles of working with yeast

In Hungarian, *kelt tészta* (risen dough) is the term used for all baked goods in which yeast is used as the rising agent. It includes all breads and sweet or savoury pastries.

Care must be taken when preparing risen dough in order to obtain a light, spongy result which will taste wonderful and be easy to digest. If the proper procedures are not followed, the final product risks being coarse and heavy.

# Starters

Put the fresh yeast or empty the sachets of dry yeast into a bowl. Add about 1/4 cup tepid water and a pinch of sugar and shake the bowl for a few seconds until all the yeast is covered with water. The mixture should start to bubble within 5 minutes. Make sure that the water is just tepid. As yeast is a living substance, hot water will kill it whereas cold water will inhibit its growth. The ideal temperature is 38–39°C – slightly warmer than body temperature. You can set the bowl in a warm-water bath to encourage the yeast to bubble.

# Kneading

While an electric mixer equipped with a dough hook for kneading your dough will certainly make life easier, it is, however, important to learn the method for kneading by hand to give you a better understanding of and feel for working with dough.

Put the dough in a large bowl and knead using the knuckles and thumb of one hand. The knuckles penetrate deeply into the dough, moving in a circular direction. Pull the dough upwards with the thumb and fingers of the same hand, and alternate these two actions – kneading and pulling the dough. You can rotate the bowl with your free hand to achieve the circular motion. As you add the fat to the dough, the dough becomes less sticky and will come away from the hand you are using to knead it.

A quantity of dough made of 1kg of flour requires about 10 minutes' kneading. If using an electric mixer, 5 minutes should suffice.

The bowl of an electric mixer is not large enough to contain more than 1kg of flour and all the other ingredients. When using more than 1kg of flour, mix all the ingredients in a large bowl and transfer half into a mixing bowl. After 5 minutes' kneading, remove the dough and knead the second half of the mixture. When both halves are kneaded, combine them, mixing by hand before setting them aside to rise.

Some yeast doughs are quite soft. At first, you may find them difficult to handle but it is their very softness that ensures the light spongy texture of the finished product. After 8 minutes of hand kneading, add a little oil and knead for another 2 minutes. This will also serve to clean your hand of any sticky dough. If the dough is very stiff, 1–2 teaspoons of whisky or vodka can be added to soften it.

When you have finished kneading the dough, sprinkle it with flour or rub a little oil over its entire surface, then cover the bowl with a clean cloth.

# Proving the Dough

The dough needs warm surroundings to rise successfully. The easiest way to maintain an even temperature is to place the bowl containing the dough in a warm-water bath.

If soft dough is not baked for several hours after it has risen, it can turn sour. This can be prevented by punching the dough down and storing it in the refrigerator.

When you are ready to bake it, bring it back to room temperature then allow it to rise again before proceeding.

# Shaping the Dough

Turn out the risen dough onto your board or work surface.

If you tilt the bowl and sprinkle a little flour into the gap between the dough and the inside of the bowl, this will make it easier to turn out. The turned-out dough should be lightly covered in flour. It can then be divided into portions which you can keep on the edge of the board until ready to roll out.

When rolling out your dough, try not to work with a heavy hand and avoid applying excessive pressure. Use light, even movements when shaping the dough.

Keep a small heap of flour at the edge of your board and sprinkle your work surface and rolling pin generously with the flour.

Dip your cookie cutters into the flour regularly to prevent them sticking to the dough.

After scraping the flour off your board with a dough scraper, use a damp disposable paper towel to clean the work top.

## Glazing

To glaze your cake and give its top an appetising sheen, make the following washes:

For cakes baked with milk and butter, brush the top with sour cream thinned with a few drops of water.

For all other cakes and cookies use either beaten whole egg or just beaten egg white.

Sour cream gives a result that is softer than the glaze obtained using egg wash.

# Baking

Never put risen dough into a very hot oven because the crust will harden first, leaving the inside raw. A well-baked loaf or cake should be light and of a uniform golden colour.

# Cooling

Chocolate and other fillings always tend to seep out of the dough during baking. So it is a good idea to turn the pastry out of the baking tin as soon as it comes out of the oven and while it is still hot. As it cools, the liquid chocolate solidifies, attaching the pastry to the tin and making it difficult to turn out without breaking.

Cool the pastry on a rack to allow air to circulate around it.

Pour hot water into the baking tins immediately after removing the pastry. This dissolves the baked-on residue and saves you time and effort when washing up.

# Delicious Light Dough Cakes

## Plain Challah (or Kalacs)

In a typical Jewish home every festive meal begins with two loaves of *challah.* Under an embroidered cover the *challot* are arranged on a special plate which is only brought out for these festive occasions. The head of the family makes a blessing over them, elevating the meal to a symbolic ceremony of thanksgiving. The participants at the table receive a slice of the sanctified *challah.* The atmosphere is always warm and hallowed.

We have many traditions, but not all of them are kept by all of us. As this is such a beautiful tradition held at the arrival of our Sabbath, week after week, we all like to observe it.

Makes two large or three small loaves.

**3 cups warm water pinch of sugar**
**20g fresh or 1 sachet dry yeast**
**1kg plain flour**
**1 level teaspoon salt**
**4 tablespoons vegetable oil**

**egg wash for glazing (optional)**

Put 1/4 cup of the water, pinch of sugar and the yeast in a deep bowl. Stand the bowl in a warm-water bath. It should take 8–10 minutes for the yeast to bubble and the rising action to begin.

Once the yeast has risen, pour the rest of the water over it and add the flour and the salt, mixing all the ingredients together either by hand or with a wooden spoon. Knead for 2–3 minutes by hand using the method described on page 11 or using the hook attachment of your electric mixer.

Add 2 tablespoons of the oil, reserving the rest for the end of the kneading process. Knead by hand for a further 10 minutes, or 5 minutes in the electric mixer. Sprinkle a small amount of flour over the dough or rub it with a table-spoon of oil and cover with a clean cloth.

Keep it in a warm place or place bowl in warm water. Let the dough rise for 1 hour or until it doubles in size.

Punch down the dough and knead it again with the remaining oil. Leave it to rise again for 20 minutes.

Preheat the oven to 210°C.

When the dough is risen, place it on a well-floured board. Knead again, then divide the dough into two or three parts, according to the amount of loaves you are making.

The dough can be braided using one of the following methods (method given is for two loaves, but can easily be adapted for three):

1. Take half of the dough and divide it into three equal parts. Roll these into three balls. Using the palms of your hands, roll each ball

into a 30cm rope, thicker in the centre and tapering towards each end. Once you have rolled out the three ropes, lay them out vertically in front of you and, starting with the ends farthest from you, plait the three strands in the same manner that you would braid hair. Secure the ends by pinching them together and folding them under the braid. Repeat this process with the other half of the dough.

2. Take half of the dough and divide it into four equal parts and roll them into balls. Using the palms of your hands, roll each ball into a rope 30cm long and 2.5cm thick. Lay them side by side on your work surface and join them at one end by pinching the strands together.

Number them 1 to 4 (from left to right). Braid by threading 1 over 2, under 3 and over 4.

Repeat this action until the braid is complete. Secure the ends by pinching them together and folding them under the braid. Repeat this process with the other half of the dough.

3. Pinch off a third of the dough. Form the larger section comprising the other two thirds into a long loaf. Make a deep cut in the top of the loaf and set aside. Divide the smaller section into three parts, roll them into small ropes and braid them as described in method 1. Place the braid over the cut on the long loaf, and

pinch in the ends to secure it firmly (this will prevent it from slipping off during baking).

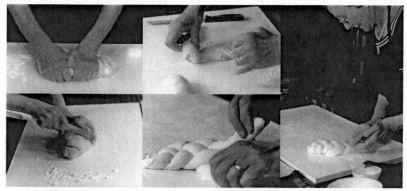

Carefully transfer the braided loaves to a well-floured or oiled baking tray, according to your preference. Brush them with either beaten egg or warm water in which you have dissolved a few grains of sugar. Leave the loaves to rise for 25 minutes.

Bake for 45–50 minutes. (See "Chapter 4".)

# Sweet Challah

Makes two or three loaves.

**2 3/4 cups warm water**
**1/2 cup caster sugar**
**20 fresh or 1 sachet dry yeast**
**1kg plain flour**
**1 level teaspoon salt**
**1 egg plus 2 egg yolks**
**4 tablespoons vegetable oil**

Put 1/4 cup of the water, a pinch of the sugar and the yeast into a deep bowl and sprinkle with a little of the flour. Stand the bowl in a warm-water bath. It should take 8–10 minutes for the yeast to bubble and rising action to begin. Once the yeast has risen, pour the rest of the water over it and add the remaining flour, sugar, salt and egg, mixing all the ingredients together either by hand or with a wooden spoon. Knead by hand using the method described on page 11 or using the hook attachment of your electric mixer.

Knead for 2–3 minutes, then add the oil, reserving a little of the oil to add at the end of the kneading process. Knead by hand for 10 minutes, or 5 minutes in the electric mixer. Sprinkle a small amount of flour over the dough or rub it with a tablespoon of oil and cover with a clean cloth.

Keep it in a warm place or place the bowl in warm water. Let the dough rise for 1 hour or until it doubles in size.

Punch down the dough and knead it again with 2 tablespoons of oil. Leave it to rise again for 20 minutes.

Preheat the oven to 210°C.

When risen, place the dough on a well-floured board, knead again, then divide it into two equal parts. Braid the dough as you would for Plain *Challah,* see page 16.

Carefully transfer the braided loaves to a well-floured or oiled baking tray. Brush them with either beaten egg or warm water in which you have dissolved a few grains of sugar. Leave them to rise for 25 minutes.

Bake for 45–50 minutes.

## Delectable Filled Rolls (Ooga)

The basic sweet milk dough and fillings in this recipe can be used in different ways to make delicious pinwheels and other shapes as well as the rolls below. Makes two large rolls.

**1/4 cup warm water**
**pinch of sugar**
**20g fresh or 1 sachet dry yeast**
**1 1/4kg plain flour at room temperature**
**3 cups warm milk**
**3/4 cup brown sugar**
**1 teaspoon salt**
**120-150g sour cream (full- or low-fat),**
 **slightly warmed**
**70g butter, slightly warmed**

## *Chocolate Filling (quantity for one roll)*

**2 heaped teaspoons cocoa powder**
**3/4 cup brown sugar**

# Poppy Seed Filling (quantity for one roll)

**1 cup water**
**1/2 cup caster sugar**
**200g ground poppy seed**
**grated rind of 1 lemon**

# Cinnamon Filling (quantity for one roll)

**1 tablespoon cinnamon**
**1/2 cup caster sugar**
**1/2 cup sultanas**

**sour cream for glazing**

To make the dough, pour 1/4 cup of warm water, pinch of sugar and the yeast into a deep bowl. Sprinkle a little flour onto the contents of the bowl.

Put the bowl in a warm place or in a warm-water bath. It should take 8–10 minutes for the yeast to bubble.

Add all the warm milk, brown sugar and sour cream to the risen yeast. Mix in the flour and salt, either by hand or with a wooden spoon, and knead for 2–3 minutes, either by hand or in an electric mixer. Do not be alarmed at the softness of the dough.

Add the warmed butter, kneading and pulling the dough for 10 minutes and rotating the bowl, as described on page 11. If you are using an electric mixer, knead for 5 minutes on speed 3–4 using the dough hook attachment. Knead the dough until it comes away from the sides of the bowl.

Sprinkle a little flour over the dough or rub it with a little oil, cover it with a clean cloth and set aside to rise in a warm place or in a warm-water bath for 1 hour or until it has doubled in size.

While the dough is rising, make the chocolate, poppy seed and/or cinnamon filling.

To make the chocolate filling, mix the cocoa and brown sugar together in a small bowl.

To make the poppy seed filling, pour the water into a saucepan, add the sugar and bring to the boil. Stir in the poppy seed, reduce the heat and cook gently for 2–3 minutes adding more water if the mixture is too thick to spread. Remove from the heat, mix in the lemon rind and set aside to cool.

To make the cinnamon filling, mix the cinnamon, sultanas and sugar together in a small bowl.

Preheat the oven to 200°C.

Turn out the dough onto a well-floured work surface and divide it into two equal portions.

Gently shape the first portion into a disc. Using a rolling pin, quickly roll out the dough into a rectangle about 65x55cm in size and about 1cm thick. Spread the filling of your choice over the dough before rolling up.

Starting at the end closest to you, roll the dough up, rolling it away from you. Pull the dough, stretching it as you roll it up. Once all the dough has been rolled up, pinch the dough together along the whole length of the roll and pinch the ends closed. Repeat this process with the second portion.

Transfer each roll, seam-side down, to an oiled round baking tin and leave it to rise again for 20–30 minutes.

To glaze the rolls, brush them with a little sour cream thinned with a few drops of water.

Bake for about 1 hour, rotating the tins halfway through to ensure even browning. Both rolls can be baked at the same time.

Remove the rolls from the oven and turn out immediately. Allow to cool on a rack before cutting into thick slices. (See "Chapter 2.")

# Kato's Butter Pita

This is my husband's favourite and the recipe comes from his mother, Kato. The aroma of the butter pita baking transports him back to his mother's kitchen and awakens childhood memories. He has meticulously instructed me in the way to prepare it as his mother did, and I would like to dedicate the following recipe to her memory.

**2–3 tablespoons warm water pinch of sugar**
**8g fresh or 1 level teaspoon dry yeast**
**3/4 cup warm milk**
**scant 1/3 cup sugar**
**40–50g sour cream**
**300g plain flour**
**1/4 teaspoon salt**

**20g butter, slightly warmed**

**vegetable oil for frying**

To make the dough, pour the warm water, pinch of sugar and the yeast into a deep bowl. Sprinkle a little flour onto the contents of the bowl.

Put the bowl in a warm place or in a warm-water bath. It should take 8–10 minutes for the yeast to bubble.

Add all the warm milk, the rest of the sugar and sour cream to the risen yeast. Mix in the flour and salt, either by hand or with a wooden spoon, and knead for 2–3 minutes, either by hand or in an electric mixer. Do not be alarmed at the softness of the dough.

Add the warmed butter, kneading and pulling the dough for 10 minutes and rotating the bowl, as described on page 11. If you are using an electric mixer, knead for 5 minutes on speed 3–4 using the dough hook attachment.

Knead the dough until it comes away from the sides of the bowl. Sprinkle a little flour over the dough or rub it with a little oil, cover it with a clean cloth and set aside to rise in a warm place or in a warm-water bath for 1 hour or until it has doubled in size.

Tear tennis-ball-sized portions from the risen dough. Lightly flour your work surface and roll each ball out to form a thin round disc, the size of an entree plate.

In a frying pan, heat a little oil and cook the discs until they are golden brown on both sides, pricking them with the tines of a fork as they cook.

Serve with a bowl of reduced-fat sour cream on the side and enjoy with hot coffee.

Delectable Filled Rolls

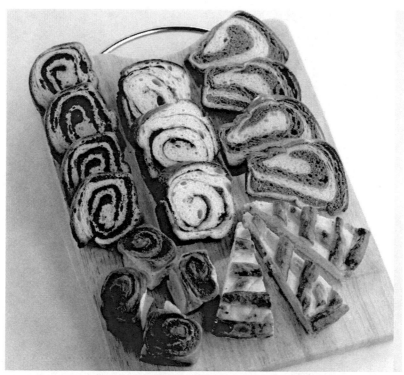

Clockwise from top right: Chocolate Kugelhopf, Lattice Cheesecake, Chocolate Pinwheels, Delectable Filled Rolls with poppy seed and chocolate fillings

Chocolate Pinwheels

Walnut Pinwheels

# Chocolate Pinwheels (Rozsa)

If butter pita is my husband's favourite, this is everyone else's. My children named these chocolate pinwheels *rózsa,* the Hungarian word for 'rose'. (The 'zs' is pronounced as the second g in garage.) The fragrance of baking *rózsa* was always guaranteed to entice the neighbourhood children into my kitchen with all their friends in tow.

To make the recipe even more wicked, dot the centre of each roll with a pea-sized dab of butter before baking.

**sweet milk dough for Kato's Butter Pita, See section entitled "Kato's Butter Pita"**

## *Filling*

**1/2 cup caster sugar**
**1 heaped teaspoon cocoa powder**

Preheat the oven to 200°C.

Shape the risen dough into a ball without overworking it. Sprinkle your work surface with flour and, using a rolling pin, roll out a long thin rectangle 25x75cm, with the long side parallel to the edge of your work surface.

Mix the sugar and cocoa powder together in a small bowl, then distribute the mixture evenly over the entire surface of the dough.

Roll the dough up tightly into a long sausage, beginning with the edge closest to you and rolling away from you. Leave the roll to rest for 10–15 minutes. The filling will melt slightly inside the warm dough.

Slice the roll into sections about 4cm thick. Arrange them with the flat side facing upwards on a well-oiled or paper-lined baking dish, touching each other. As they bake they will join together and the chocolate will seep out creating a rich and shiny bottom crust. Bake for 25–30 minutes. Remove from the oven and turn the *rózsa* out onto a rack to cool.

To serve, separate the *rózsa* by hand and arrange on a platter. (See "Chapter 2.")

# Walnut Pinwheels

**sweet milk dough for Kato's Butter Pita, See section entitled "Kato's Butter Pita"**

## *Filling*

**6 heaped tablespoons ground walnuts**
**1/2 cup caster sugar**
**grated rind of 1 lemon**

Preheat the oven to 200°C.

Shape the risen dough into a ball without overworking it. Sprinkle your work surface with flour and, using a rolling pin, roll out a long thin rectangle 25x75cm, with the long side parallel to the edge of your work surface.

Mix the walnuts, sugar and lemon rind together in a small bowl, then distribute the mixture evenly over the entire surface of the dough.

Roll the dough up tightly into a long sausage, beginning with the edge closest to you and rolling away from you. Leave the roll to rest for 10–15 minutes.

Slice the roll into sections about 4cm thick. Arrange them with the flat side facing upwards on a well-oiled or paper-lined baking dish, touching each other. Bake for 25–30 minutes. Remove from the oven and turn the pinwheels out onto a rack to cool.

To serve, separate the pinwheels by hand and arrange on a platter. (See "Chapter 2.")

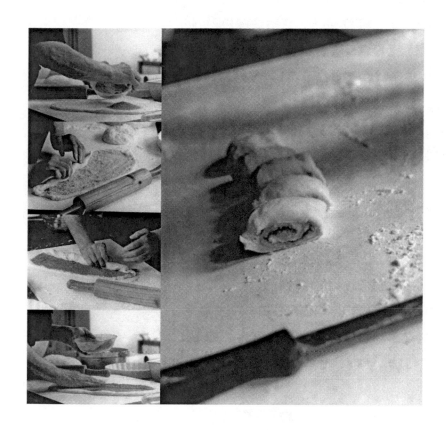

# Chocolate Kugelhopf

l/4 cup warm water
pinch of sugar
20g fresh or 1 sachet dry yeast (reserve
 5g fresh or 1 level teaspoon dry for filling)
1 1/2 cups warm milk
1/2 cup brown sugar
1 level teaspoon salt
100g sour cream, slightly warmed
500g plain flour
50-80g butter, slightly warmed
2 tablespoons vegetable oil

## Filling

5g fresh or the 1 level teaspoon dry yeast
l/4 cup warm milk
2 teaspoons cocoa
2 tablespoons plain flour
1/3 cup brown sugar

sour cream for glazing

To make the dough, pour 1/4 cup of warm water, pinch of sugar and the yeast into a deep bowl. Sprinkle a little flour onto the contents of the bowl.

Put the bowl in a warm place or place it in a warm-water bath. It should take 8–10 minutes for the yeast to bubble. Add the warm milk, sugar, salt and sour cream to the risen yeast. Mix in the flour, either by hand or using a wooden spoon, and knead for 2–3 minutes, either by hand or in an electric mixer. Add the warmed butter, kneading and pulling the dough for 10 minutes and rotating the bowl as described on page 11. If you are using an electric mixer, knead for 5 minutes on speed 3–4. Knead the dough until it comes away from the sides of the bowl.

Take one third of the dough and set aside. Sprinkle a little flour over the remaining dough or rub it with a little of the oil, cover it with a clean cloth and set aside to rise in a warm place or in a warm-water bath.

To make the filling, dissolve the yeast in the warm milk. Mix in the cocoa, flour and sugar and add to the reserved dough. Knead until the cocoa mixture has been thoroughly incorporated into the dough and it is a uniform dark colour. Sprinkle with a little flour or rub with oil and set aside in a warm place to rise. After 1 1/2 hours, when both portions of dough have doubled in size, add the reserved oil to the white dough and knead to incorporate it thoroughly. This should take 2–3 minutes.

Preheat the oven to 200°C.

Roll it out on a floured work surface to a thickness of 1cm.

Roll out the chocolate-flavoured dough or simply shape it with your hands to the same size as the rolled-out white dough. Place it on top of the white dough. Starting at the end closest to you, roll up the dough, rolling away from you. Pull the dough, stretching it as you roll it up. Once all the dough has been rolled up, pinch it together, the whole length of the roll, and press the ends closed. Transfer the roll to an oiled *kugelhopf* tin and leave it to rise again for 20–30 minutes.

To glaze the rolls, brush them with a little sour cream thinned with a few drops of water.

Bake for 50 minutes, rotating the baking dish after 25 minutes to ensure even browning.

Remove the cake from the oven and turn it out onto a rack to cool. (See "Chapter 2.")

# De Luxe Kugelhopf

The following three *kugelhopfs* are variations on the same theme. They are richer, sweeter and more elaborate than the previous chocolate version. I prepare them on special occasions, such as parties and important family gatherings, when I want to lash out and not worry about counting calories.

**20g fresh or 1 sachet dry yeast**
**3/4 cup warm milk**
**160g melted butter**

**100g caster sugar**
**5 egg yolks**
**130g ground almonds salt**
**400g plain flour**

**egg wash for glazing**

In a small bowl, dissolve the yeast in 1/4 cup of the warm milk and set aside in a warm-water bath for 8–10 minutes until it starts to bubble. Pour the remaining warm milk into a large bowl and add the risen yeast, butter, sugar, egg yolks, ground almonds and salt, mixing well before adding the flour. Mix with a wooden spoon for about 5 minutes until everything is well blended or use an electric mixer on speed 3.

Preheat the oven to 200°C.

Transfer the mixture to an oiled *kugelhopf* mould, making sure that the mould is not more than half full, otherwise the mixture will overflow. Set aside to rise in a warm place or in a warm-water bath for 30 minutes. Brush the top with some egg wash.

Bake for 40–45 minutes.

Remove the cake from the oven, turning it out onto a rack to cool.

# Sultana Kugelhopf

**20g fresh or 1 sachet dry yeast**

**1 cup warm milk**
**150g softened butter**
**100g caster sugar**
**3 egg yolks**
**1/4 teaspoon salt**
**450g flour**
**150g sultanas**

**egg wash for glazing**

In a small bowl, dissolve the yeast in 1/4 cup of the warm milk and set aside in a warm-water bath for 8–10 minutes until it starts to bubble. Pour the remaining warm milk into a large bowl and add the risen yeast, butter, sugar, egg yolks and salt, mixing well before adding the flour. Mix with a wooden spoon for about 5 minutes until everything is well blended or use an electric mixer on speed 3. Add the sultanas, kneading to distribute them evenly through the mixture.

Preheat the oven to 200°C.

Transfer the mixture to an oiled *kugelhopf* mould, making sure that the mould is not more than half full, otherwise the mixture will overflow. Set aside to rise in a warm place or in a warm-water bath for 30 minutes. Brush the top with some egg wash.

Bake for 40–45 minutes.

Remove the cake from the oven, turning it out onto a rack to cool.

# Almond Kugelhopf

**20g fresh or 1 sachet dry yeast**
**1 cup warm milk**
**140g softened butter**
**100g caster sugar**
**6 egg yolks**
**100g sour cream**
**1/4 teaspoon salt**
**600g plain flour**

## *Filling*

**150g ground almonds**
**100g caster sugar**
**grated rind of 1/2 lemon**
**1 tablespoon vanilla sugar**

**egg wash for glazing**

In a small bowl, dissolve the yeast in 1/2 cup of the warm milk and set aside in a warm-water bath for 8–10 minutes until it starts to bubble. Pour the remaining warm milk into a large bowl and add the risen yeast, butter, sugar, egg yolks, sour cream and salt, mixing well before adding the flour. Mix with a wooden spoon for about 5 minutes until everything is well blended or use an electric mixer on speed 3.

Mix all the ingredients for the filling in a bowl.

Preheat the oven to 200°C.

Transfer the mixture to an oiled *kugelhopf* mould to a depth of 3cm. Sprinkle generously with the almond mixture. Repeat this process ending with a layer of the batter, making sure that the mould is not more than half full, otherwise the mixture will overflow. Set aside to rise in a warm place or in a warm-water bath for 30 minutes. Brush the top with some egg wash.

Bake for 40–45 minutes.

Remove the cake from the oven, turning it out onto a rack to cool.

# Golden Dumpling Cake

This cake turns any dinner into a festive event. It is easy to assemble and relatively quick to make. My grandchildren call it 'caveman's cake', as you tear it apart into dumpling-sized pieces with your hands instead of cutting it with a knife.

**20g fresh or 1 sachet dry yeast**
**pinch of sugar**
**1 3/4 cups warm water**
**50g caster sugar**
**1/4 teaspoon salt**

**1 egg**
**600g plain flour**
**50g margarine**

**apricot jam**
**vegetable oil**

## *Filling*

**100g ground walnuts**
**80g caster sugar**
**grated rind of 1 lemon**

To make the dough, dissolve the yeast and pinch of sugar in 1/4 cup of warm water in a large bowl. Cover and set aside to rise for 5 minutes or until the yeast starts to bubble.

Add the remaining water, sugar, salt and egg to the bowl, mixing with a wooden spoon. Add the flour, mixing to incorporate it into the other ingredients, and knead for about 4 minutes. Add the margarine and knead for an additional 3 minutes. The dough should be quite soft.

Sprinkle a little flour over the dough or rub it with a little oil. Cover it with a clean cloth and set aside to rise in a warm place or in a warm-water bath for 1 hour or until doubled in size.

While the dough is rising, make the filling. Mix the ground nuts, caster sugar and lemon rind together in a small bowl.

Preheat the oven to 200°C.

Turn out the dough onto a well-floured board. Shape into a flattened disc, sprinkle it with flour and either roll it out with a rolling pin or simply stretch it out with your hands to a thickness of 1.5cm. Cut into rounds with a 5cm cookie cutter or a wine glass, dipping the cutter into some flour from time to time to prevent the dough sticking to it.

Collect the left-over dough, kneading it together and rolling it out until it has all been cut into rounds.

Thoroughly grease a 25cm square or round baking tin, covering the bottom and sides. Arrange one layer of the rounds in the baking tin, touching each other. Place a 1/4 teaspoon of apricot jam on each round, then cover the whole surface with half the filling and sprinkle lightly with drops of oil.

Cover with a second layer of dough, spreading with jam, the remaining filling and sprinkling with oil.

Cover the second layer with the remaining rounds of dough and a sprinkling of oil. If there are not enough rounds of dough left, just stretch the ones you have to cover the surface.

Set aside to rise in a warm place for 30 minutes.

Bake for 45–50 minutes.

Remove the cake from the oven and turn it out onto a serving dish. Serve within an hour of baking.

To serve, tear pieces from the cake and enjoy while it is still warm.

# Doughnuts

Once I gave this recipe to a friend. The next time I met her she told me that her doughnuts had turned out much better than mine. When I asked her how she had managed to improve on my recipe, she replied that she had replaced the single egg in my recipe with 3 egg yolks.

It is easy to make recipes richer but I think that the following one produces a good-tasting doughnut which is also deliciously light.

**15g fresh or 1 heaped teaspoon dry yeast**
**pinch of sugar**
**1 3/4 cups warm water**
**50g caster sugar**
**1/4 teaspoon salt**
**1 egg**
**500g plain flour**
**50g margarine**

**vegetable oil for frying**

## *To Serve*

**caster sugar**
**pricot jam**

To make the dough, dissolve the yeast and the pinch of sugar in 1/4 cup of warm water in a large bowl. Cover and set aside for 5 minutes or until the yeast begins to bubble.

Add the remaining water, sugar, salt and egg, mixing with a wooden spoon.

Add the flour, mixing to incorporate it into the other ingredients and knead for about 4 minutes. Add the margarine and knead for an additional 3 minutes.

The dough should be quite soft.

Sprinkle a little flour over the remaining dough or rub it with a little oil. Cover it with a clean cloth and set aside to rise in a warm place or in a warm-water bath for 1 hour or until doubled in size.

Turn out the dough onto a well-floured board. Shape into a flattened disc, sprinkle it with flour and either roll it out with a rolling pin or simply stretch it out with your hands to a thickness of 1.5cm. Cut into rounds with a 5cm cookie cutter or a wine glass, dipping the cutter into some flour from time to time to prevent the dough sticking to it.

Collect the left-over dough, kneading and rolling it out until it has all been cut into rounds.

Cover the rounds and set them aside to rise for 10 minutes.

Prepare a bowl with the sugar and a slotted spoon for retrieving the doughnuts. Heat the oil in a deep saucepan or frying pan. Drop the doughnuts into the hot oil, a few at a time, leaving them room to expand. Cover the pan and fry for about a minute, making sure that the oil does not get too hot. Uncover and turn the doughnuts, allowing them to cook for a few more seconds. When they are golden brown all over, retrieve them with a slotted spoon and sprinkle them with the sugar, which will adhere to their hot surface. Repeat this process until all the doughnuts have been fried. You may need to add extra oil during the frying, as the doughnuts will absorb a little.

Transfer to a serving platter and serve with small bowls of jam on the side.

# Sweet Butter and Cheese Cakes

This category of cakes has a denser consistency than the previous one. The fat can be incorporated into the flour either by hand or in an electric mixer using the K beater on minimum speed for 2 minutes. With these recipes, it is difficult to specify an exact amount of liquid. The dough should be just soft enough to be kneaded easily. Add 1/2 cup of warm milk at first, adding more if a softer consistency is required.

## Chimney-Sweep Rolls

This is a good recipe to start experimenting with this type of dough. The rolls are quick and easy to make, yet they look and taste delicious.

**15g fresh or 1 sachet dry yeast**
**l/4 cup warm water**
**pinch of sugar**
**80g butter, softened**
**300g plain flour**
**1 egg yolk**
**50g sugar**
**1/8 teaspoon salt**
**1/2 cup warm milk**

## Filling

**50g butter**
**60g sugar**
**30g cocoa**

**beaten egg white for glazing**

Dissolve the yeast in the warm water with a pinch of sugar. Cover and set aside to rise for 8–10 minutes in a warm-water bath.

In a large bowl, work the butter into the flour with your fingers until it resembles coarse breadcrumbs. This can also be done with an electric mixer, using the K beater on minimum speed for 2 minutes. Add the risen yeast, egg yolk, sugar, salt and milk, mixing well with your hand or a wooden spoon. Knead lightly for 6–8 minutes. The dough should be firm but elastic. If you find it hard to knead, add a little more milk.

Cover and set aside to rise for 30–40 minutes in a warm-water bath.

While the dough is rising, make the filling.

Cream the butter with the sugar, then add the cocoa, mixing thoroughly.

Preheat the oven to 200°C.

Roll out the dough to a thickness of 3mm. Spread the filling evenly over the entire surface of the dough. Cut the dough into 8cm squares.

Take a square and place it with one corner facing you. Roll it up away from you until the corners make a diamond shape on each side. Repeat this process with all the remaining squares of dough. Transfer the rolls to a baking sheet that has been well oiled or lined with baking paper, brush them with the beaten egg white and set aside to rise for 10 minutes.

Bake for 25–30 minutes, rotating the baking sheet after 15 minutes to ensure even browning. You may need to reshape the rolls during baking. (See "Chapter 3.")

Chimney-Sweep Rolls

Cockscombs

Kindli with walnut and poppy seed fillings

Flaky Crescents

# Flaky Crescents (Pozsonyi Kifli)

This recipe calls for two glazing operations, the first with egg yolk and the second with egg white, to produce the traditional cracked glaze of *Pozsonyi kifli.* They take their name from the Hungarian name for Bratislava – the current capital of Slovakia.

**15g fresh or 1 heaped teaspoon dry yeast**
**pinch of sugar**
**1/4 cup warm water**
**200g margarine**
**500g plain flour**
**1/4 cup orange juice or sweet wine**
**1 egg yolk**
**3 medium potatoes, boiled and mashed**
**2 tablespoons sugar**
**1/2 teaspoon salt**

**apricot jam**

## *Nut Filling*

**1 egg white**
**100g sugar**
**juice of 1/2 lemon**
**rind of 1/2 lemon**
**150g ground walnuts or almonds**
**1/4 Granny Smith apple, grated**

# *Poppy Seed Filling*

**1 cup water**
**1/2 cup sugar**
**250g freshly ground poppy seed**
**grated rind of 1/2 lemon**

**beaten egg yolk for glazing**
**egg white for glazing**

Dissolve the yeast and the pinch of sugar in the warm water and set aside to bubble for 5 minutes.

Work the margarine into the flour with your fingers until it resembles coarse breadcrumbs. Add the risen yeast, juice or wine, egg yolk, mashed potatoes, sugar and salt, mixing them together by hand to form a soft dough. Knead, bringing the dough in from the sides of the bowl and pushing it into the middle with your knuckles. If you find the dough too stiff to knead, add more wine until it is soft enough to work. Continue to knead for 5–6 minutes, then cover and set aside to rest for 30–40 minutes.

While the dough is rising, make the fillings.

To make the nut filling, beat the egg white and sugar together, add the lemon juice and rind, then mix in the ground nuts and grated apple.

To make the poppy seed filling, put the water and sugar into a small saucepan and heat until the water dissolves. Add the poppy seed, stirring well, and simmer for a few minutes. Remove from the heat and add the lemon rind. If the mixture is too dense, add a little more water.

Preheat the oven to 200°C.

Turn the dough out onto a floured work surface and divide it into 5 equal portions. Roll out each portion into a disc 25–30cm in diameter. Spread a thin layer of jam over the entire surface.

Cut the disc into 8 equal segments.

Place 1 teaspoon of the filling onto the outer edge of each segment, then roll it up towards the centre. Repeat until all the dough and filling has been used. Arrange the rolls on a paper-lined baking sheet and brush them with the beaten egg yolk.

Allow to rest for 10 minutes then brush with the unbeaten egg white. Bake for 25–30 minutes or until they are golden brown, rotating the baking sheet after 15 minutes to ensure even browning. (See "Chapter 3.")

# Sour-Cream Crescents

**20g fresh or 1 sachet dry yeast**
**pinch of sugar**
**1/4 cup warm milk**
**150g butter or margarine, slightly warmed**
**450g plain flour**
**150g sour cream**
**3 teaspoons caster sugar**
**1/2 teaspoon salt**

## *Filling*

**thick jam such as powidl**
**or pitted prunes**

**sour cream for glazing**
**vanilla sugar**

Preheat the oven to 200°C.

To make the dough, dissolve the yeast and pinch of sugar in the warm milk. Cover and set aside to rise for 5 minutes.

Work the butter or margarine into the flour until it resembles coarse breadcrumbs, then add the sour cream, sugar, salt and yeast mixture, mixing rapidly but thoroughly. Knead for 3–4 minutes to obtain a firm but elastic dough. Set aside to rest for 30 minutes.

On a lightly floured work surface, roll out the dough to a disc 4mm thick. Using a large, round cookie cutter, cut out dough circles. Put either a teaspoon of jam or a pitted prune in the centre of each circle and fold over to form a crescent shape. Seal the edges by pressing them down with the tines of a fork. Arrange them on a paper-lined baking sheet and brush them with some sour cream thinned with a few drops of water.

Leave to rest for 30 minutes before baking for 25–30 minutes, or until golden brown. Remove from the oven and roll them in vanilla sugar while still hot.

# Butter Buns (Pogácsa)

When butter buns are good, they are very good. The only thing wrong with them is that they are so very more-ish.

**20g fresh or 1 sachet dry yeast**
**2 tablespoons warm water**
**pinch of sugar**
**125g softened butter**
**125g margarine**
**700g plain flour**
**2 egg yolks**
**1/2 cup caster sugar**

**1/2 teaspoon salt**
**1/2–3/4 cup warm milk**
**200g sour cream**

**beaten egg white for glazing**

Put the yeast into a small bowl and add the warm water and pinch of sugar. Leave to rise in a warm place for 8–10 minutes.

In a large bowl, work the butter and margarine into the flour with your fingers until it resembles coarse breadcrumbs. Add the risen yeast, egg yolks, sugar, salt, milk and sour cream, mixing well with your hand or a wooden spoon.

Knead for 6-8 minutes, bringing the dough in from the edges with your fingers and pushing it down into the centre of the bowl with your knuckles. Rotate the bowl with your free hand as you knead. Alternatively, knead for 4 minutes in an electric mixer using the K beater.

If the dough is hard to knead, add a little more warm milk until it reaches the desired consistency. It should be firm but elastic.

Cover and set aside to rise for 30–40 minutes in a warm-water bath.

Turn the dough out onto a floured work surface and knead it again, shaping it into a ball. Roll it out into a rectangle 40x50cm. Fold one third of the dough to cover the middle third and then over again so that three layers are formed.

Cover with a cloth and allow to rest for 30 minutes.

Roll out the dough to a thickness of about 1–1.5cm.

Preheat the oven to 200°C.

Taking care not to cut through the dough, score a criss-cross pattern into its surface with a sharp knife.

Press out discs with a 5cm cookie cutter. Place on a baking sheet lined with baking paper, leaving about 1cm between the discs. Knead the left-over dough into a ball, roll it out and score, pressing out discs until all the dough has been used. Brush the discs with some beaten egg white to glaze, and allow to rest for 20 minutes.

Bake for 25–30 minutes or until golden brown, rotating the sheet after 15 minutes to ensure even browning. (See "Chapter 4.")

# Snake Roll

The following recipe is for one of those Hungarian cakes which are best served when still warm.

If you are using low-fat cottage cheese for the filling, the addition of 4 tablespoons of low-fat sour cream will improve its flavour.

This roll can also be filled with the nut or poppy seed filling described on page 49 or simply with some excellent thick fruit preserve.

**20g fresh or 1 sachet dry yeast**
**pinch of sugar**
**2 tablespoons warm water**
**2 tablespoons sugar**
**250g margarine**
**1/2 cup orange juice**
**1 whole egg plus 1 egg yolk**
**1/8 teaspoon salt**
**500g plain flour**

## Cheese Filling

**1 egg**
**1/2 cup brown sugar pinch of salt**
**2 tablespoons semolina or white**
 **breadcrumbs**
**500g cottage cheese.**
**grated rind of 1/2 lemon**

## Apple Filling

**5–6 apples, peeled and sliced**
**100g sugar**
**grated rind of 1 lemon**
**1 teaspoon cinnamon**

**1 cup sweet cookie crumbs, plain white breadcrumbs or ground walnuts.**

**beaten egg white for glazing**

To make the dough, dissolve the yeast and pinch of sugar in the warm water. Cover and set aside to bubble for 5 minutes.

In a deep bowl, cream the sugar with margarine. Add the orange juice, egg and egg yolk, salt, risen yeast and, last of all, the flour. Mix well and set aside to rest for 15–20 minutes.

While the dough is resting, prepare the fillings.

To make the cheese filling, combine the egg and sugar in a bowl. Stir in the salt and semolina or breadcrumbs, then add the cottage cheese and lemon rind, mixing well.

To make the apple filling, simmer the apples with the sugar until most of the liquid exuded by the apples has evaporated and the mixture is quite dry. Allow to cool and stir in the lemon rind and cinnamon. Before spreading this filling over the dough, first sprinkle it with the cookie crumbs, breadcrumbs or ground nuts to absorb any more moisture that may be exuded during baking.

Preheat the oven to 200°C.

Turn the dough out onto a floured work surface and divide into four equal portions.

Roll out each portion into a rectangle 40x25cm.

Following the illustration, cut a fringe into the two opposite sides of the rolled-out dough. Arrange the filling in the centre of the dough and fold the fringe strips over one another, bringing the dough in first from the right-hand side and then from the left, creating a patterned lattice effect over the filling.

Repeat with the other three portions of dough.

Transfer the rolls to a paper-lined baking sheet.

Brush with the beaten egg white and set aside to rest for 10 minutes. Bake for 30–35 minutes or until golden brown, rotating the baking sheet after 15 minutes to ensure even browning.

To serve, cut into slices on the diagonal.

# Cockscombs Filled with Nuts or Poppy Seeds

If you are baking cockscombs to eat after a festive meal, substitute the dough below for the dough used for making *Kindli,* see section entitled "Kindli". This will make these scrumptious cakes *parve* (suitable after eating meat).

**20g fresh or 1 sachet dry yeast**

**2 tablespoons warm milk**
**pinch of sugar**
**125g softened butter (plus 2 tablespoons**
 **for folding)**
**125g margarine**
**700g plain flour, at room temperature**
**2 egg yolks**
**1/2 cup caster sugar**
**1/2 teaspoon salt**
**1/2–3/4 cup warm milk**
**200g sour cream, warmed**
**apricot jam**

## Filling

**nut or poppy seed filling for Flaky**
 **Crescents, see "Chapter 3"**
**beaten egg white for glazing**

Put the yeast in a small bowl and add the warm milk and sugar. Leave to rise in a warm place for 8–10 minutes.

In a large bowl, work the butter and margarine into the flour with your fingers until it resembles coarse breadcrumbs. Add the risen yeast, egg yolks, sugar, salt, milk and sour cream, mixing well with your hand or a wooden spoon. Knead for 6-8 minutes, bringing the dough in from the edges with your fingers and pushing it down into the centre of the bowl with your knuckles. Rotate the bowl with your free hand as you knead.

If the dough is hard to knead, add a little more of the warm milk.

Cover and set aside to rise for 30-40 minutes in a warm-water bath.

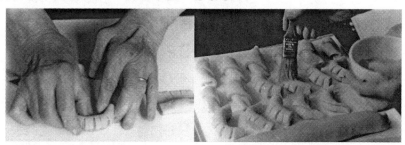

Once the dough has risen, turn it out onto a floured work surface and knead it again. Using the heel of your hand, stretch it out. Bring each end in towards the centre. Repeat this process, shape the dough into a ball, cover and set aside to rest for 30 minutes.

Roll it out until it is about 50x50cm in size. Brush it with some of the reserved soft butter. Fold one third of the dough to cover the middle third and then over again so that three layers are formed. Fold in half again from the top edge back towards you.

Cover with a cloth and allow to rest for 10 minutes. Roll out and fold again as described above and allow to rest for another 10 minutes.

Preheat the oven to 200°C.

Divide the dough into four equal portions. Roll out a portion to a thickness of about

3–4mm and spread the entire surface with apricot jam.

With a sharp knife, cut 8cm squares by first cutting strips 8cm wide along the length of the dough and then cutting similar strips crosswise.

Put a teaspoon of the prepared filling on the upper third of each square. Cut a 2cm fringe into the whole length of its lower edge. Roll up starting from the upper edge and bend into a crescent shape so that the cuts forming the fringe open up slightly. Repeat with the other three portions until all the dough has been rolled and filled.

Transfer the cockscombs to an oiled baking sheet. Brush them with beaten egg white and set aside to rest for 15 minutes.

Bake for 20–30 minutes or until golden brown, rotating the baking sheet after 15 minutes to ensure even browning. (See "Chapter 3.")

# Kindli

This traditional cake comes from northwest Hungary. It is usually baked for festivals and other special occasions and there are many recipes for both the dough and filling, all of which are delicious. This is another family favourite and even though it is not difficult to make, I save it for very special occasions.

Makes four rolls, two with poppy seed and two with walnut filling.

**15g fresh or 1 heaped teaspoon dry yeast**
**50g sugar**
**3 tablespoons warm water**
**140g margarine**
**350g plain flour**
**1 egg yolk**
**l/4 cup orange juice**
**pinch of salt**
**apricot jam**

## Filling

**nut or poppy seed filling for Flaky**
 **Crescents, See "Chapter 3"**

**egg wash for glazing**

Dissolve the yeast and a pinch of the sugar in the warm water and set aside to bubble for 5 minutes.

Work the margarine into the flour with your fingers until it resembles coarse breadcrumbs. Add the risen yeast, egg yolk, orange juice, the remaining sugar and salt, mixing by hand to form a dough. Knead, bringing the dough in from the sides of the bowl and pushing it into the middle with your knuckles. The dough should be firm but elastic. If it is too stiff, add a little more orange juice. Continue to knead for 5–6 minutes, then cover and set aside to rest for 30 minutes.

Preheat the oven to 200°C.

Divide the risen dough into four equal portions.

In turn, roll each portion out into a rectangle 35x45cm. Spread a thin layer of the apricot jam over the entire surface. Using a metal spatula or knife, spread a 2–3mm layer of filling over the layer of jam.

Roll up tightly and press the long side and both ends to seal and enclose the prepared filling. When all four portions of dough have been rolled out and filled, transfer them, seam-side down, to a baking sheet that has been lined with baking paper or well oiled.

Brush with beaten egg and set aside to rest for 10–15 minutes. Prick with a fork at 2.5cm intervals on the diagonal to form a decorative pattern.

Bake for 30–35 minutes or until golden, rotating the baking sheets after 15 minutes to ensure even browning.

Remove from the oven and allow to cool before cutting, on the diagonal, into 1.5–2cm slices. (See "Chapter 3.")

# Meringue Rolls

These should be started the day before you wish to eat them. The dough is kept in the refrigerator overnight.

**25g fresh or 1 sachet dry yeast**
**pinch of sugar**
**2 tablespoons warm water**
**2 egg yolks**
**200g margarine**
**300g plain flour**
**1 tablespoon caster sugar**
**pinch of salt**
**1 teaspoon vanilla essence**

**2 egg whites**
**1/2 cup caster sugar**
**l/4 teaspoon cream of tartar**

To make the dough, dissolve the yeast and pinch of sugar in the warm water. Cover and set aside to rise for 5 minutes.

Separate the eggs and reserve the whites in a covered bowl for use the next day. Work the margarine into the flour with your fingers until it resembles coarse breadcrumbs. Add the egg yolks, risen yeast, the tablespoon of sugar, salt and vanilla essence, mixing by hand. Knead the dough for 3–4 minutes, then transfer to a floured plastic bag and store in the refrigerator overnight.

The following day, remove the dough from the refrigerator and let it soften for 30 minutes.

Set the bowl of reserved egg whites in a warm-water bath for a few minutes. Beat the egg whites until they form soft peaks, gradually adding 1/2 cup of sugar and cream of tartar. Continue to beat until stiff peaks are formed.

Preheat the oven to 190°C.

Turn out the dough onto a floured work surface and divide into three portions. Roll one portion of the dough out to a thickness of 3mm. Spread one third of the beaten egg whites evenly over its entire surface and roll it up carefully. With a sharp knife, cut it into 2–3cm rounds. Arrange them on a baking sheet that has been well oiled or lined with baking paper. Repeat this process with the remaining two portions of dough.

Bake for 12–15 minutes or until the meringue starts to colour.

Remove from the oven before it becomes too brown.

# Rachel's Rolls

My mother used to bake these little gems to perfection. In fact, everything she baked was pleasing both to the eye and the palate. I would like to honour her memory by naming them after her.

**20g or 1 heaped teaspoon dry yeast**
**pinch of sugar**
**2 tablespoons warm water**
**250g butter or margarine**
**500g plain flour**
**4 egg yolks**
**1/4 cup orange juice**
**1/4 cup caster sugar**
**1/4 teaspoon salt**
**grated rind of 1 lemon**

**50g margarine**
**apricot jam**

# Filling

**nut filling for Golden Dumpling Cake, see "Chapter 3", with the addition of 1/4 cup sultanas**

**beaten egg white for glazing**

To make the dough, dissolve the yeast and pinch of sugar in the warm water. Cover and set aside to rise for 5 minutes.

In a large bowl, work the butter or margarine into the flour with your fingers until it resembles coarse breadcrumbs. Add the risen yeast, egg yolks, orange juice, sugar, salt and lemon rind, mixing by hand.

Knead for 5–6 minutes. Cover with plastic wrap and chill in the refrigerator for 30 minutes.

Remove from the refrigerator and roll out into a square 40x40cm. Spread the entire surface with the 50g margarine and roll up into a sausage shape.

Cover with the plastic wrap and return to the refrigerator for 25 minutes.

Remove the dough from the refrigerator and divide into 5 equal portions. Roll out the first portion into a disc 25cm in diameter. Cut the disc into 8 equal segments.

Spread each segment with a thin layer of apricot jam and the prepared nut filling. Take the outer edge of each segment and roll it up towards the centre. Repeat until all the dough and filling has been used.

Arrange the rolls on a paper-lined baking sheet and brush them with the beaten egg white.

Bake for 25–30 minutes or until they are golden brown, rotating the baking sheet after 15 minutes to ensure even browning.

Lattice Cheesecake

Jam Cornets

Lady's Caprice

Cheese Turnovers

# Cheese Turnovers (Sweet)

**20g fresh or 1 sachet dry yeast**
**2 tablespoons warm water**
**pinch of sugar**
**125g softened butter**
**125g margarine**
**700g plain flour, at room temperature**
**2 egg yolks**
**1/2 cup caster sugar**
**1/2 teaspoon salt**
**1/2–3/4 cup warm milk**
**200g sour cream, warmed**

## *Cheese Filling*

**If you are using low-fat cottage cheese,**
**the addition of 4 tablespoons low-fat**
**sour cream will improve its flavour.**

**500g cottage cheese**
**1 egg plus 1 egg white**
**1/2 cup brown sugar**
**pinch of salt**
**2 tablespoons semolina or white**
**breadcrumbs**
**grated rind of 1 lemon**

**beaten egg white for glazing**
**vanilla sugar (optional)**

To make the dough, put the yeast into a small bowl and add the warm water and sugar. Leave to rise in a warm place for 8–10 minutes.

In a large bowl, work the butter and margarine into the flour with your fingers until it resembles coarse breadcrumbs. Add the risen yeast, egg yolks, sugar, salt, milk and sour cream, mixing well with your hand or a wooden spoon.

Knead for 6-8 minutes, bringing the dough in from the edges with your fingers and pushing it down into the centre of the bowl with your knuckles. Rotate the bowl with your free hand as you knead.

You can also mix the dough in an electric mixer for 4 minutes using the K beater. If the dough is hard to knead, add a little more warm milk until it reaches the desired consistency. It should be firm but elastic.

Cover and set aside to rise for 30–40 minutes in a warm-water bath.

While the dough is rising, make the cheese filling. Mix all the ingredients together in a bowl to obtain a smooth mixture.

Preheat the oven to 200°C.

Turn the risen dough out onto a floured work surface and knead for 2–3 minutes. Cover it with a clean cloth and set aside to rest in a warm place for 20 minutes.

Turn out the dough and divide it into two parts.

On a floured work surface, roll out the first half of the dough to a thickness of 5mm. Cut 7cm strips along the length of the dough and repeat crosswise. This will give you 7cm squares of dough. Put a heaped teaspoon of the cheese filling in the centre of each square. Gather up the four corners, bringing them into the centre and pinching them tightly.

Repeat this process with the second half of the dough.

Transfer the turnovers to a baking sheet that has either been oiled or lined with baking paper. Brush them with beaten egg white and set aside to rest for 10–20 minutes.

Bake for 25–30 minutes or until golden brown in colour, rotating the sheet after 15 minutes to ensure even browning.

If desired, sprinkle some vanilla sugar over the turnovers while they are still hot. (See "Chapter 3.")

# Lattice Cheesecake

**20g fresh or 1 heaped teaspoon dry yeast**
**2 tablespoons warm water**
**pinch of sugar**
**80g softened butter**
**80g margarine, warmed**
**500g plain flour**
**2 egg yolks**
**3 tablespoons caster sugar**
**1/4 teaspoon salt**
**l/4 cup warm milk**
**150g sour cream, warmed**

## *Filling*

**600g cottage cheese**
**1/2 cup brown sugar**
**4 tablespoons sour cream**
**1 whole egg plus 1 egg yolk**
**2 tablespoons semolina or white breadcrumbs**
**grated rind of 1 lemon**

**apricot jam (optional)**
**1/2 cup white breadcrumbs (optional)**

**beaten egg white for glazing**
**vanilla sugar (optional)**

To make the dough, put the yeast into a small bowl and add the water and sugar. Leave to rise in a warm place for 8–10 minutes.

In a large bowl, work the butter and margarine into the flour with your fingers until it resembles coarse breadcrumbs. Add the risen yeast, egg yolks, sugar, salt, milk and sour cream, mixing well with your hand or a wooden spoon. Knead for 6–8 minutes, bringing the dough in from the edges with your fingers and pushing it down into the centre of the bowl with your knuckles. Rotate the bowl with your free hand as you knead.

If the dough is hard to knead, add a little more warm milk until it reaches the desired consistency. It should be firm but elastic.

Cover and set aside to rise for 30–40 minutes in a warm-water bath.

While the dough is rising, make the filling.

Mix all the ingredients for the filling together in a bowl until thoroughly combined.

Preheat the oven to 200°C.

Once the dough has risen, turn it out onto a floured work surface and knead it again. Using the heel of your hand, stretch it out. Bring the outer edges in towards the centre. Repeat this process, shape the dough into a ball, cover and set aside to rest for 30 minutes.

Pinch off one third of the dough.

On a floured work surface, roll out the dough to the shape of your baking tin (30x22cm). Ease the dough into the pan, allowing it to come up high enough to contain the cheese filling.

If desired, brush the dough with some apricot jam and sprinkle with the breadcrumbs before filling with the cheese mixture.

Spread the cheese mixture evenly over the dough.

Roll out the reserved dough to a thickness of 5mm. Cut strips with a fancy pie cutter and arrange them to form a lattice over the top of the filling. The lattice can also be formed using pencil-width rolls of dough instead of the strips.

If you prefer, you can simply roll out the remaining dough and drape it over the filling to form a closed crust, making sure that you join it to the bottom layer of dough by pinching the two edges together. Prick the crust all over with a fork to allow any steam to escape.

Glaze the top crust or lattice with the beaten egg white and bake for 40–50 minutes, rotating after 15 minutes to ensure even browning.

If desired, sprinkle the top with vanilla sugar. (See "Chapter 2, 3.")

# Jam Cornets (Hamentaschen or Oznei Haman)

These are special cakes baked for the Feast of Purim which commemorates Jewish Queen Esther's saving of her people from destruction by the wicked Haman. In Hebrew, their name means 'Haman's ears'. It is traditional to give gifts to the poor and send trays of sweetmeats including these cakes to all one's friends during the Feast of Purim.

**5g fresh or 1 level teaspoon dry yeast**
**pinch of sugar**
**2 tablespoons warm water**
**150g margarine**
**250g plain flour**
**100g caster sugar**
**2 eggs**
**rind of 1/2 lemon**

## *Filling*

**thick jam such as *powidl***
**or poppy seed or nut filling for Flaky**
 **Crescents, see "Chapter 3"**

**beaten egg white for glazing**

To make the dough, dissolve the yeast and pinch of sugar in the warm water. Cover and set aside to bubble for 5 minutes.

In a large bowl, work the margarine into the flour with your fingers until it resembles coarse breadcrumbs. Add the risen yeast, sugar, eggs and lemon rind, mixing well. Knead for 3–4 minutes, then set aside in a warm place to rise for 25–30 minutes.

Preheat the oven to 200°C.

Turn out the dough onto a floured work surface and roll it out to a thickness of 3mm.

Cut out circles with a large round cookie cutter. Put a generous spoonful of your preferred filling in the centre of each circle and roll into a cornet shape.

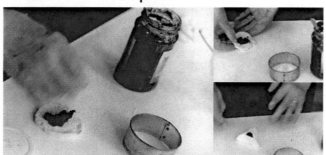

Place each cornet on a paper-lined baking sheet.

Brush with the beaten egg white and set aside to rise for 20 minutes.

Bake for 25–30 minutes or until golden brown, rotating the baking sheet after 15 minutes to ensure even browning. (See "Chapter 3.")

# Nut Slice

**20g fresh or 1 heaped teaspoon dry yeast**
**pinch of sugar**
**2 tablespoons warm water**
**120g margarine**
**500g plain flour**
**4 egg yolks**
**80g icing sugar**
**1/4 teaspoon salt**
**1/4 cup orange juice**

## *Filling*

**150g ground almonds or hazelnuts**
**120g sugar**
**grated rind of 1 lemon**

## *Topping*

**4 egg whites**
**100g icing sugar**
**100g ground hazelnuts**
**grated rind of 1 lemon**
**1 tablespoon plain flour**

**4 tablespoons apricot jam, slightly warmed**

To make the dough, dissolve the yeast and pinch of sugar in the warm water. Cover and set aside to rise for 5 minutes.

In a large bowl, work the margarine into the flour with your fingers until it resembles coarse breadcrumbs. Add the egg yolks, risen yeast, sugar, salt and orange juice, mixing by hand.

Knead rapidly for 3–4 minutes. The dough should be firm but elastic. If it is too stiff, add a little more orange juice.

Cover and set aside to rise in a warm place for 30 minutes.

While the dough is rising, make the filling and the topping.

To make the filling, mix the ground nuts, sugar and lemon rind together in a small bowl.

To make the topping, beat the egg whites to form stiff peaks, gradually adding the sugar. Carefully fold in the nuts, lemon rind and flour.

Preheat the oven to 200°C.

Grease a 30x20cm baking dish or line it with baking paper.

Divide the dough into three portions. Roll out each portion to fit snugly into the baking dish, letting the dough come 1cm up the sides of the dish.

Sprinkle half of the filling evenly onto the first portion of dough in the baking dish and cover it with the second piece of dough. Spread this with the remaining filling and cover with the third piece of dough. Prick with the tines of a fork at regular intervals to allow any steam to escape.

Set aside to rest for 15 minutes.

Bake for 20 minutes. Remove from the oven and spread the top of the slice with the apricot jam.

Spread the prepared topping evenly over the layer of jam and return the slice to the oven, reduced to 175°C, for a further 20 minutes.

Remove the slice from the oven and allow it to cool before turning it out onto a rack.

To serve, cut into squares.

# Gerbeaud Slice

A little slice of history ... this popular treat takes its name from Emil Gerbeaud, a famous confectioner and chocolate factory owner who came from Paris to Budapest, Hungary in the 1880s and whose lavish Cafe Gerbeaud still operates in that city to this day.

**15g fresh or 1 heaped teaspoon dry yeast**
**pinch of sugar**
**3 tablespoons warm water**

**120g unsalted butter or margarine**
**300g plain flour**
**1/2 cup orange juice**
**3 egg yolks**
**40g icing sugar**
**1/4 teaspoon salt**

## Filling

**3 egg whites**
**1/2 cup caster sugar**
**150g ground walnuts**

## Chocolate Glaze

**4 tablespoons water**
**1/4 cup icing sugar**
**1 teaspoon unsalted butter or margarine**
**1 tablespoon cocoa powder**
**80g dark chocolate, melted**

**3 tablespoons smooth apricot jam,**
 **slightly warmed**

To make the dough, dissolve the yeast and pinch of sugar in the warm water. Cover and set aside to rise for 5 minutes.

Work the butter or margarine into the flour with your fingers until it resembles coarse breadcrumbs. Add the risen yeast, orange juice, egg yolks, sugar and salt, mixing by hand.

Knead for 3–4 minutes. The dough should be firm but elastic. Cover and set aside to rise in a warm place for 30–40 minutes.

While the dough is rising, make the filling and the glaze.

To make the filling, beat the egg whites to form stiff peaks, gradually adding the sugar. Carefully fold in the walnuts.

To make the glaze, heat the water in a small saucepan with the sugar and butter and, when the butter has melted, stir in the cocoa powder and chocolate. Stir over a very low heat for 5 minutes. Set aside to cool slightly.

Grease a 35x25cm baking dish or line it with baking paper.

Preheat the oven to 200°C.

Divide the dough into three portions. Roll out each portion to fit snugly into the baking dish, letting the dough come 1cm up the sides of the dish.

Spread a thin layer of jam over the entire surface of the dough in the baking dish and then spread half of the filling evenly over the top. Cover with the second piece of dough. Spread this with the remaining jam and filling and cover with the third piece of dough. Prick the top with the tines of a fork at regular intervals to allow any steam to escape.

Bake for 35–40 minutes, rotating the tin after 15 minutes to ensure even cooking.

Remove from the oven and allow the slice to cool before turning it out onto a rack. Using a spatula, spread an even layer of the glaze over the top of the slice and allow this to become completely cold before cutting.

# Lady's Caprice

**10g fresh or 1 level teaspoon dry yeast**
**pinch of sugar**
**2 tablespoons warm water**
**100g unsalted butter or margarine**
**300g plain flour**
**2 tablespoons orange juice**
**2 egg yolks**
**2 tablespoons caster sugar**
**pinch of salt**

## *Topping*

**2 egg whites**
**120g caster sugar**
**1 level teaspoon cream of tartar**

**apricot jam**
**flaked almonds**
**melted chocolate**

To make the dough, dissolve the yeast and pinch of sugar in the warm water. Cover and set aside to rise for 5 minutes.

Work the butter or margarine into the flour with your fingers until it resembles coarse breadcrumbs. Add the risen yeast, orange juice, egg yolks, sugar and salt, mixing by hand.

Knead for 3–4 minutes. The dough should be firm but elastic. Cover and set aside to rise in a warm place for 20–25 minutes.

Preheat the oven to 200°C.

Grease a 30x20cm baking dish.

Roll out the dough to fit snugly into the baking dish.

Bake for 15–20 minutes so that the dough is partially baked.

In the meantime, prepare the topping.

Beat the egg whites, gradually incorporating the cream of tartar and sugar, until the egg whites form stiff peaks.

Remove the partially baked crust from the oven. Spread with the apricot jam, cover with the prepared topping and sprinkle evenly with the flaked almonds. Reduce the heat to 175°C and bake the cake for an additional 15–20 minutes until the topping has set and is lightly coloured.

Melt the chocolate and either dip the tines of a fork into it and make a diagonal design over the top of the cake, or transfer the molten chocolate to an improvised piping bag made from silver foil and make the design in that manner.

When the cake is completely cool, cut into thin rectangular slices. (See "Chapter 3.")

# Savoury Buns and Sticks

## Light Sour-Cream Buns

**25g fresh or 1 teaspoon dry yeast**
**2 tablespoons warm milk**
**pinch of sugar**
**100g butter or margarine**
**350g plain flour**
**1 egg yolk**
**100g sour cream**
**1 tablespoon sugar**
**1/3 teaspoon salt**

**50g softened butter or margarine**

**beaten egg white for glazing**

Dissolve the yeast in the warm milk with the pinch of sugar. Cover and set aside in a warm place to prove for 5 minutes.

Work the butter or margarine into the flour with your fingers until it resembles coarse breadcrumbs. Add the risen yeast, egg yolk, sour cream, sugar and salt, mixing by hand to form a soft dough. Knead for 5 minutes and set aside to rest in the refrigerator for 30 minutes.

Turn the dough out onto a floured work surface and roll it out into a 30cm square. Spread half of the softened butter evenly over its surface, then fold the left-hand third of the dough into the middle and then the right-hand third over it so that three layers are formed.

Cover and return to the refrigerator to rest for 20 minutes.

Repeat this process, rolling, spreading with butter and folding, returning the dough to the refrigerator for a final 10 minute rest.

Preheat the oven to 200°C.

Turn the dough out onto a floured work surface and roll out to a thickness of 1.5cm. Press out rounds with a cookie cutter and arrange them on a paper-lined baking sheet.

Glaze with the beaten egg white and set aside to rise for an additional 10 minutes.

Bake for 30–35 minutes, rotating the baking sheet after 20 minutes to ensure even baking.

Butter Buns

Plain Challah, and Boiled Bagels

Potato Brioches

Potato Fingers sprinkled with caraway seeds and salt

# Paprika Buns

**20g fresh or 1 sachet dry yeast**
**2 tablespoons warm milk**
**pinch of sugar**
**250g butter or margarine**
**400g plain flour**
**1 egg yolk**
**150g sour cream**
**100g grated hard cheese, such as**
 **cheddar or parmesan**
**1 teaspoon sweet paprika**
**1 level teaspoon salt**

**beaten egg white for glazing**

Dissolve the yeast in the warm milk with the pinch of sugar. Cover and set aside in a warm place to prove for 5 minutes.

Work the butter or margarine into the flour with your fingers until it resembles coarse breadcrumbs. Add the risen yeast, egg yolk, sour cream, grated cheese, paprika and salt, mixing by hand to form a soft dough. Knead for 5 minutes and set aside to rest for 1 hour.

Preheat the oven to 200°C.

Turn the dough out onto a floured work surface and roll out to a thickness of 1cm. Score to form a criss-cross pattern. Press out rounds with a cookie cutter and arrange them on a paper-lined baking sheet.

Glaze with the beaten egg white and allow to rise for an additional 30 minutes. Bake for 30–35 minutes, rotating the baking sheet after 20 minutes to ensure even baking.

Remove from the oven and eat warm or at room temperature.

# Cheese Buns

**20g fresh or 1 sachet dry yeast**
**2 tablespoons warm milk**
**pinch of sugar**
**250g butter or margarine**
**500g plain flour**
**2 egg yolks**
**200g sour cream**
**200g grated cheese, such as cheddar**
**10g grated hard cheese, such as**
 **parmesan**
**1/2 teaspoon salt**

**beaten egg white for glazing**
**extra grated hard cheese**

Dissolve the yeast in the warm milk with the pinch of sugar. Cover and set aside in a warm place to prove for 5 minutes.

Work the butter or margarine into the flour with your fingers until it resembles

coarse breadcrumbs. Add the risen yeast, egg yolks, sour cream, both kinds of grated cheese and salt, mixing by hand to form a soft dough. Knead for 5 minutes and set aside to rest for 1 hour.

Preheat the oven to 200°C.

Turn the dough out onto a floured work surface and roll out to a thickness of 1cm. Press out rounds with a cookie cutter and arrange them on a paper-lined baking sheet.

Glaze with the beaten egg white, sprinkle thickly with grated hard cheese and allow to rise for an additional 30 minutes. Bake for

30–35 minutes, rotating the baking sheet after 20 minutes to ensure even baking.

Remove from the oven and eat warm or at room temperature.

# Onion Rolls

**15g fresh or 1 heaped teaspoon dry yeast**
**3 tablespoons warm water**
**pinch of sugar**
**1/2 cups warm water**
**3 tablespoons oil**
**2 tablespoons sugar**
**1/2 teaspoon salt**
**500g plain flour**
**1 medium onion, grated**
**1 teaspoon curry powder**
**freshly ground white pepper**
**pinch of salt**

**beaten egg white for glazing**

Dissolve the yeast in the warm water with the pinch of sugar. Cover and set aside in a warm place to rise for 5 minutes.

Pour the water, oil, sugar, salt and all the flour into a large bowl. Mix with a wooden spoon and then knead for 5–7 minutes. Cover and set aside to rise in a warm place for 1 hour.

Punch down and mix in the onion, curry powder, salt and pepper to taste.

Preheat the oven to 200°C.

Pinch off tennis-ball-sized portions of dough and roll them into balls.

Arrange them on a paper-lined baking sheet, leaving 1.5cm distance between them.

Brush them with the beaten egg white and leave to rest for 10 minutes.

Bake for 35–45 minutes or until golden brown, rotating the baking sheet after 20 minutes to ensure even baking.

# Boiled Bagels

**10g fresh or 1 heaped teaspoon dry yeast**
**1 teaspoon sugar**
**1 cup warm water**
**1/4 teaspoon salt**
**1 tablespoon vegetable oil or 1 teaspoon margarine**
**300g plain flour**

**egg wash for glazing**
**poppy or sesame seeds (optional)**

In a large bowl, combine the yeast with a pinch of the sugar and 3–4 tablespoons of the water and set aside to rise in a warm place for 5 minutes.

When the yeast is bubbling, add the remaining water, sugar, salt, oil and flour and stir with a wooden spoon. Knead the dough by hand for 8 minutes, or in the electric mixer, using the dough hook, for 5 minutes. Remove the hook attachment from the dough and, with oiled hands, form the dough into a ball. Leaving the dough in the mixing bowl, cover it and set aside in a warm-water bath to rise for 1 hour.

Turn out the dough onto a floured work surface and knead for 2-3 minutes, then divide it into portions of about 60g. Let the portions sit for 10 minutes. To make the bagel shape, place your finger in the centre of each portion and spin once or twice until the hole is about 1.5cm across. The bagels should be about 10cm across when you have finished. Cover and leave to rise for another 10 minutes.

Preheat the oven to 200°C.

Bring a large saucepan of water to the boil with 1 teaspoon salt.

Carefully place the bagels, a few at a time, into the boiling water and simmer for 1 minute or less. Transfer them with a slotted spoon to a platter, then after a few minutes remove them to a paper-lined baking sheet.

Brush the bagels with beaten egg and sprinkle with seeds, if desired. Bake for 20–25 minutes or until golden brown. (See "Chapter 4.")

# Potato Brioches

The following three savoury buns are not only good-looking, but they also taste delicious! They are perfect for afternoon tea with a cup of coffee.

**20g fresh or 1 sachet dry yeast**
**2 tablespoons warm milk**
**pinch of sugar**
**80g butter or margarine**
**500g plain flour**
**1/2 cup warm milk**
**1 egg yolk**
**150g boiled potato, mashed**
**50g sugar**
**1/4 teaspoon salt**

**beaten egg white for glazing**
**poppy seeds (optional)**

Dissolve the yeast in the warm milk with the pinch of sugar. Cover and set aside in a warm place to rise for 5 minutes.

Work the butter or margarine into the flour with your fingers until it resembles coarse breadcrumbs. Add the risen yeast, milk, egg yolk, mashed potato, sugar and salt, mixing by hand to form a soft dough. Knead for 5 minutes, then cover and set aside to rest for 1 hour.

Preheat the oven to 200°C.

Turn the dough out onto a floured work surface and roll out to a thickness of 1cm. Cut the dough into 1cm wide strips and then cut the strips into 10cm lengths.

Taking three strips at a time, braid them into small loaves and arrange them on a paper-lined baking sheet.

Glaze with the beaten egg white and sprinkle with poppy seeds, if desired.

Allow to rise for an additional 30 minutes.

Bake for 30–35 minutes, rotating the baking sheet after 20 minutes to ensure even baking. (See "Chapter 4.")

# Hearty Potato Scones

**20g fresh or 1 sachet dry yeast**
**2 tablespoons warm milk**
**pinch of sugar**
**250g butter or margarine**
**600g plain flour**
**250g sour cream**
**2 medium potatoes, boiled and mashed**
**2 teaspoons sugar 1/2 teaspoon salt**

**beaten egg white for glazing**
**grated hard cheese, such as parmesan**

Dissolve the yeast in the warm milk with the pinch of sugar. Cover and set aside in a warm place to prove for 5 minutes.

Work the butter or margarine into the flour with your fingers until it resembles coarse breadcrumbs. Add the risen yeast, sour cream, mashed potato, sugar and salt, mixing by hand to form a soft dough. Knead for 5 minutes, then cover and set aside to rest for 1 hour.

Preheat the oven to 200°C.

Turn the dough out onto a floured work surface and roll out to a thickness of 1cm. Press out rounds with a cookie cutter and arrange them on a paper-lined baking sheet.

Glaze with the beaten egg white, sprinkle thickly with grated cheese and allow to rise for an additional 30 minutes. Bake for 30–35 minutes, rotating the baking sheet after 20 minutes to ensure even baking.

# Butter and Cottage Cheese Scones

The dough for these scones is prepared in the evening and baked the following day.

**20g fresh or 1 sachet dry yeast**
**2 tablespoons warm milk**
**pinch of sugar**
**250g butter or margarine**

**250g plain flour**
**1 large or 2 small egg yolks**
**250g cottage cheese**
**1/4 teaspoon salt**
**pinch of baking powder**

**beaten egg white for glazing**

Dissolve the yeast in the warm milk with the pinch of sugar. Cover and set aside in a warm place to prove for 5 minutes.

Work the butter or margarine into the flour with your fingers until it resembles coarse breadcrumbs. Add the risen yeast, egg yolk, cottage cheese, salt and baking powder, mixing by hand to form a soft dough. Knead for 5 minutes, then form into a loaf shape and place in a floured plastic bag. Set aside in the refrigerator overnight.

The next day, remove the dough from the refrigerator and let it come back to room temperature before shaping.

Preheat the oven to 200°C.

Turn the dough out onto a floured work surface and roll out to a thickness of 1–1.5cm. Press out rounds with a cookie cutter and arrange them on a paper-lined baking sheet.

Glaze with the beaten egg white. Bake for 30–35 minutes, rotating the baking sheet after 20 minutes to ensure even baking.

# Potato Fingers

**10g fresh or 1 teaspoon dry yeast**
**2 tablespoons warm milk**
**100g butter or margarine**
**250g plain flour**
**1 egg yolk or 2 tablespoons sour cream**
**(for the cholesterol-conscious)**
**120g baked potato, mashed**
**1/4 teaspoon salt**

**beaten egg white for glazing**

## *Toppings*

**coarse salt mixed with caraway seeds**
**or coarse salt mixed with poppy seeds**
**or grated parmesan cheese**

Dissolve the yeast in the warm milk. Cover and set aside in a warm place to prove for 5 minutes.

Work the butter or margarine into the flour with your fingers until it resembles coarse breadcrumbs. Add the sour cream or egg yolk, risen yeast, mashed potato and salt, mixing by hand and kneading rapidly to form a soft dough. Set aside in a warm place to rise for 25–30 minutes.

Preheat the oven to 200°C.

Turn out the dough onto a floured work surface. Break off pieces of the dough and roll them into lengths the thickness of a finger. Cut them into 10cm sticks. Brush them with the beaten egg white and sprinkle them with the topping of your choice.

Bake for 30 minutes or until golden brown. (See "Chapter 4.")

## Savoury Shapes

**10g fresh or 1 teaspoon dry yeast**
**1 teaspoon sugar**
**2 tablespoons warm water**
**80g butter or margarine**
**250g plain flour**
**100g sour cream**
**2 egg yolks**
**pinch of salt**

**beaten egg white for glazing**

## *Toppings*

**coarse salt mixed with caraway seeds**
**or coarse salt mixed with sesame seeds**
**or grated parmesan cheese**

Dissolve the yeast with the sugar in the warm water and set aside to bubble for 5 minutes.

Work the butter or margarine into the flour with your fingers until it resembles coarse breadcrumbs. Add the risen yeast, sour cream, egg yolks and salt, mixing by hand and kneading to form a stiff dough. Set aside in a warm place to rise for 25–30 minutes.

Preheat the oven to 200°C.

On a floured work surface, roll out the dough to a thickness of 3mm. Brush with the beaten egg white and sprinkle with the topping of your choice. Using a fluted dough cutter, cut out small diamond shapes or use a heated knife to cut out 10x1cm strips.

Transfer to a baking sheet that has been well oiled or lined with baking paper.

Bake for 30 minutes or until golden brown.

These shapes should keep well for several weeks in an airtight container.

# Wheat-B ran Cookies

**20g fresh or 1 sachet dry yeast**
**pinch of sugar**
**2 tablespoons warm milk**
**200g butter or margarine**
**350g plain flour**
**150g wheat bran**
**1 egg yolk (reserve the white)**
**250g cottage cheese**
**150g sour cream**
**120g baked potato, mashed**

**1 teaspoon salt**

**beaten egg white for glazing**

Dissolve the yeast and pinch of sugar in the warm milk. Cover and set aside in a warm place to prove for 5 minutes.

Work the butter or margarine into the flour and bran with your fingers until it resembles coarse breadcrumbs. Add the risen yeast, egg yolk, sour cream, cottage cheese and salt, mixing by hand to form a soft dough. Knead for 5 minutes, then cover and set aside to rest for 1 hour.

Preheat the oven to 200°C.

Turn the dough out onto a floured work surface and roll out to a thickness of 1–1.5cm. Press out rounds with a cookie cutter and arrange them on a paper-lined baking sheet.

Glaze with the beaten egg white. Bake for 30–35 minutes, rotating the baking sheet after 20 minutes to ensure even baking.

# Back Cover Flap

**Baba Schwartz,** a Hungarian-born baker renowned for her superb cakes and pastries, lives in Melbourne. This book is the culmination of a lifetime of baking.

# Back Cover Material

**'A delightful book ... you can almost smell a warm, yeasty kitchen aroma wafting from the pages.'—The Age**

Baking with yeast is becoming a lost art. Many cooks would love to utilise the incredible properties of yeast, but lack a guide to inform and inspire them.

*The Lost Art of Baking with Yeast* shows how simple baking with yeast can be, and how irresistible the results.

The book includes recipes for cakes, slices, pastries, buns and ... Baba's famous Golden Dumpling Cake. Baba Schwartz introduces the principles of yeast baking and gives handy hints for kneading and proving dough to perfection.

These recipes, with their distinctive Hungarian flavour, will delight your family and friends. If you love baking, you will love discovering these recipes, some unique and some classic.

Photography: Sonia Payes

# Books For ALL Kinds of Readers

At ReadHowYouWant we understand that one size does not fit all types of readers. Our innovative, patent pending technology allows us to design new formats to make reading easier and more enjoyable for you. This helps improve your speed of reading and your comprehension. Our EasyRead printed books have been optimized to improve word recognition, ease eye tracking by adjusting word and line spacing as well as minimizing hyphenation. Our EasyRead SuperLarge editions have been developed to make reading easier and more accessible for vision-impaired readers. We offer Braille and DAISY formats of our books and all popular E-Book formats.

We are continually introducing new formats based upon research and reader preferences. Visit our web-site to see all of our formats and learn how you can Personalize our books for yourself or as gifts. Sign up to Become A RHYW Registered Reader.

www.readhowyouwant.com

CPSIA information can be obtained at www.ICGtesting.com
231782LV00003B/69/P